Julian of Norwich

Simple Ladders of Perfection

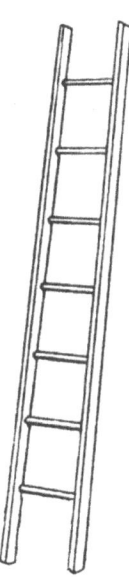

Julian of Norwich

Holy Trinity of Love

In Father, Son, and Spirit, three,
the Ground of every Trinity of love, we see
a Truth as deep, and broad, and free
as all of God's created Mystery!

And God alone, and God alone,
does all this simple and exalted sight impart
to every lovely seeking heart.

from Lo, ere the deepest waters
(C) 2001, Will Melnyk, revised 2013

Simple Ladders of Perfection

Julian of Norwich
Simple Ladders of Perfection

Walter William Melnyk

Based Upon His Contemporary Translation:
A Revelation of Divine Love

*"All shall be well, and all shall be well,
and all manner of thing shall be well."*
~ Mother Julian

Julian of Norwich

Copyright 2014
Walter William Melnyk

The text of his original translation
also copyright 2014

All Rights Reserved
No reproduction, copy, or transmission of this publication may be made without the prior consent of the author, with the exception of brief excerpts for the purpose of citation or literary review.

Printed and Bound in the United States of America
Cover Photo by Walter William Melnyk, 2014,
West Door of Norwich Cathedral

ISBN-13: 978-1500343989
ISBN-10: 1500343986

Hazelnut Press

In Blessed Memory of
Sr. Scholastica Marie, OJN
*Windblown waves of golden grass,
rolling gray storm clouds;
music of eternal bliss.*

Julian of Norwich

In the Context of the Passion

All of Julian's ten simple Ladders of Perfection, all of her spiritual joy and optimism, takes place within her visions of the Passion. These "bodily showings" are often glossed over by lovers of Julian as they search out her spiritual gems. Yet without her experience of the Passion of Christ there is no hazelnut, no goodness of God, no Motherhood of Christ, no "Love was His meaning."

Julian's Passion Narrative is recounted in four of her sixteen showings:

> The first is of His precious crowning with thorns,
> The second is of the discoloring of His fair face,
> The fourth is of the scourging of His tender body,
> The eighth is of the last pains of Christ, and His cruel dying.

They are presented on the following pages as the context for Julian's lesson of love, from "A Revelation of Divine Love: Julian of Norwich," Hazelnut Press, 2014, W.W. Melnyk, translator, chapters four, ten, twelve, and sixteen.

We must experience this Passion if we wish to understand anything that follows from it.

The Precious Crowning with Thorns

In all this, suddenly I saw the red blood trickling down from under the crown of thorns, hot, and fresh, and very plentiful. It was as if at the time of His Passion, when the crown of thorns was pressed down upon His blessed head: He, right so both God and man, who suffered thus for me. I realized, truly and mightily, that it was God, Himself, who showed me this, without any intermediary.

I saw the bodily vision continuing, with the plenteous bleeding of Christ's head. The great drops of blood fell down from under the crown, seeming like pellets as it came from His veins. And in the coming out, it was brown-red, for the blood was very thick; and in spreading across His forehead was bright red; and when it came to His brows, then it vanished.

This bleeding continued until many things were seen and understood. The fairness and lifelikeness was like nothing else. The plenteousness was like drops of water falling from the eaves in a heavy rain, that fall so thickly that no one can count them by physical means. As for the roundness, it was like scales of herring spreading across His forehead. These three images come to my mind: pellets, for roundness, flowing from His veins; herring scales, for roundness, in spreading across His forehead; drops from the eaves for unmeasurable plenty. This showing was lively and real, horrible and awful, sweet and lovely.

Simple Ladders of Perfection

The Discoloring of His Fair Face

After this I had a bodily sight of the face upon the crucifix that hung before me, in which I beheld continuously another part of His Passion: contempt, spitting and defiling, pummeling and much continuous pain, more than I can describe; and His face often changing color.

At one time I saw how half His face was overrun with dried blood, from the ear to the middle. Then the other half was covered in the same way, and then again the first part. I saw this in a bodily vision, sorrowfully and darkly

The Scourging of His Tender Flesh

After this I saw another revelation, beholding Christ's body bleeding profusely, as it were by the scourging, like this: His fair skin was cut very deeply into His tender flesh, as from a sharp lashing all over His sweet body. The hot blood ran out so profusely that I could see neither skin nor wound, but only the blood. But when the blood came to where it would have fallen from the body, there it vanished. Even so, the bleeding continued for a while, until it could be seen with careful scrutiny. It was so plenteous, it seemed to me, that I thought had it been actually happening naturally and in the flesh for all that time, the whole bed would have been soaked in blood, and the blood spilled all over.

His Last Pains and Cruel Death

After this, Christ showed a portion of His Passion near to His death. I saw His sweet face, as it was, dry and bloodless with a deathly pallor; and then more pale yet, deathly, languishing; then turning an even more deathly blue, then more brown-blue, as the flesh turned more deathly yet. Thus His Passion was shown to me most vividly in His precious face, and especially in His lips. There I saw the appearance of these four colors, though at first they were lively, ruddy, and pleasant to my sight. It was a sorrowful change, to see this deep dying.

And His nose shriveled and dried out, as I saw it, and the sweet body was brown and black, all changed from His fair, living color into dry dying. For in that very time that our Lord and blessed Savior died upon the cross I saw there was a dry, harsh, and terribly cold wind blowing. And when the precious blood had completely bled out and passed from His sweet body, there yet remained some moisture in the sweet flesh of Christ. The painful drying and blood loss within, and the harsh wind and cold coming from without, met together in Christ's sweet body. These four things, two within and two without, dried the flesh of Christ over time. And though this pain was bitter and sharp, it was also long lasting, as I see it. And painfully it dried up all the living fluids of His flesh. Thus I saw the sweet flesh die, bit by bit, drying out with unimaginable pains. And as long as there was any spirit of life in Christ's flesh, so long did He suffer those pains.

This drawn out pain was as though he had been seven nights at the point of passing away, dying, dead. By this I mean that His sweet body was so discolored, so dry, so shriveled, so deathly, and so piteous that it looked as though He had been dead for a week, yet still continually dying. I thought the dying of Christ's flesh was the last, and worst, pain of His Passion.

This dying brought to my mind Christ's words, "I thirst." I saw Christ in a double thirst: one physical, and the other spiritual (which I will speak of in the thirty-first chapter,) These words He spoke of the bodily thirst, which I understood was caused by the drying up of moisture, for His blessed flesh and bones were left alone without any blood or moisture. The blessed body dried alone for a long time, with twisting of the nails because of the weight of the body.

As I understood, because of the tenderness of the sweet hands and feet, and the grievously large, hard nails, the wounds waxed wider, and the body sagged under its weight from hanging there such a long time, and the piercing and wringing out of the head under the binding of the crown, all covered with dried blood, sweet hair clinging to His head, and the dried flesh to the thorns, and the thorns to the dying flesh.

At first, while the flesh was alive and bleeding, the continual pressure of the thorns made the wounds wide. And furthermore, I saw that the sweet skin and the tender flesh, with the hair and the blood, was all pulled out and loosened from the bone by the thorns, as though it were slashed in many pieces, hanging like a cloth that would soon fall off because it was so heavy and loose while it still had the weight of natural moisture. That filled me with great fear and sorrow, for I thought I would not want to see it fall from Him even to save my life. How this was done I could not see, but I knew it was because of the sharp thorns and the cruel and grievous setting of the crown upon His head unsparingly, without pity.

This sight continued awhile. Then it began to change, and I looked and wondered how it might be. And then I saw it all began to dry out, and the crown lost some of its weight. And thus it was wrapped all about, as it were crown upon crown. The crown of thorns was stained with the blood, and also the crown of His head, all one color, like clotted blood when it has dried. The skin of His flesh, which showed upon his face and body, was covered with small wrinkles, and tanned in color like a dried board when it is old and burned, and the face was more brown than the body.

Thus I saw four kinds of dryings: The first was bloodlessness, the second was the pain that followed from that, the third was hanging out in the air as men hang up a cloth to dry, and the fourth was that His natural body begged for moisture, but no comfort was ministered to Him in all His distress and woe.

Ah! Hard and grievous was His pain! But how much harder and more grievous it was when the moisture failed, and all was dried up and thus hanging. These were the pains I saw in His blissful head: the first was the onset of the dying while the body was yet moist; the other, more slowly, His dried out flesh hanging as the wind blowing about Him dried Him out even more, with cold pains, than my heart can imagine. And I saw other pains also, beyond my ability to describe, for there are no words . . .

This showing of Christ's pains filled me with pain also, for though I knew well He suffered only once, yet He showed it to me [so dramatically] that it filled my mind, as I had asked. And through all this pain, the only pains I felt were Christ's pains. And I thought, "Little did I know what pain it was that I had asked for." And in my wretchedness I repented of my request, thinking that if I had known what it would be I would have been loath to pray for it. For I thought the pains it caused me surpassed even bodily death.

Thus I saw our Lord Jesus lingering a long time, for His union with the Godhead gave strength to His manhood to suffer, for love, more than all men can suffer. By this I mean not only more pain than all men might suffer now, but also that He suffered more pain than all men of salvation who ever lived, from the beginning until the last day, might be able to think or imagine

And with this, our good Lord said with great bliss, "Lo, how I loved you."

Julian of Norwich

The Ladder of Perfection

The fourteenth century in England, known mostly for plagues and barbarism, was a watershed in the development of Christian mystical spirituality. The "English Mystics," among them Walter Hilton, Richard Rolle, Julian of Norwich, and the Authors of The Cloud of Unknowing and the Anchoress' Rule, introduced a new spiritual egalitarianism into the Christian Faith where the authoritarianism of Holy Church had held sway for centuries. They emphasized personal spirituality and the possibility of an unmediated (mystical) experience of God; a breath of fresh air in the midst of the long era (c. 1100-1700) of Medieval Scholasticism, and such heavy theological thinkers as Albertus Magnus, Duns Scotus, William of Ockham, Bonaventure and Thomas Aquinas.

A breath of fresh air they might have been, but they were also dangerous. If the ordinary individual could have a personal, unmediated experience of God, where was the need for Holy Church? If an ordinary Christian could experience the Beatific Vision alone in her room or anchorhold, where was the need for the preaching and teaching of Clergy, most especially of Bishops? So along with their vivid descriptions of visions (Julian describes three kinds: bodily sight, words formed in her understanding, and spiritual knowing) they took great care to warn, guide, and caution their readers and disciples.

Hilton might be described as the systematic theologian of the English Mystics. His ascetical theology (the theological foundation for a life of prayer) rivals the Scholastics in depth, scope, and learning. And in order to prevent ordinary folks from straying too far from the faith and practice of Holy Church, he gives us in his book (The Scale of Perfection) a carefully described ladder upon which the untrained might safely climb to heaven. His work is often described as the first English language work of ascetical and mystical theology. Very nearly within moments he was followed by many others, Dame Julian of Norwich among them.

Hilton's Ladder of Perfection describes the steps by which a soul attains union with God, as if it were a guidebook:

* The soul is reformed in the Image of God, first in faith only, then also in experience

* There follows a "dark night" in which all consolation disappears, and the soul is cleansed of earthly desires and led to desire the love of God

* Finally the soul becomes immersed in God, and thereby attains perfection.

An Augustinian monk for much of his life, Hilton was well read, and relied upon the works of many earlier writers. Yet he mentioned in his own writing that he, himself, had never experienced any of the sublime familiarity with God that he describes in The Ladder.

Julian was quite the opposite. As a lay woman (likely before and after she entered her anchorhold (hermitess cell,) she had less access to great theological libraries. She described herself as "unlettered." Whether that means she had no academic degree after her name, could not read Latin, or was indeed illiterate, we cannot know. But she was wise, and learned her Scripture and Tradition somewhere. Hilton, a leader in the Church, is remembered by name. Julian, an ordinary Christian, is remembered only by the name of the patron saint of the church building to which her cell was attached.

What dramatically sets Julian apart from Hilton is that she did have a set of vivid visions (she calls them showings or revelations) in which she experienced God as "homely" and "courteous" ~ at once intimately familiar, and formally chivalric. Her work, a Revelation of Divine Love, is a description of that experience. Unlike Hilton, she gives us no practical guidance for how, or where, or when to pray. Where Hilton is rational, Julian is emotional; where he is speculative, she is affective. So much so that it is often said Julian gives us no step by step instruction, no Ladder of Perfection. But this is to forget that a period of some theological learning took place before her Revelations, and a lifetime of theological reflection afterwards as her book was being written. So we do well to pay attention to her words.

There are indeed ten Ladders of Perfection in Julian's writing, and they are wonderfully evident once you have decided to look for them. They do not build upon each other, but are different ways of expressing the spiritual ascent. Perhaps because the Holy Trinity is so important to Julian's thought, each simple Ladder is a little Trinity of three steps.

In this book, each of her ladders is set in the midst of well-known proverbs, aphorisms, or quotations from her work (with the chapters where they are found noted in parentheses.) The Ladders and quotations are not grouped into separate topics or subject areas. Hilton might have done that, or Aquinas, but not Julian. In this book all is set down in the order in which she wrote. Sometimes it will be easy to see her progression of logic. Often it will not be easy. Julian is trying to express in words, for our benefit, what she knows to be inexpressible. A train of thought may be interrupted by a vision; a showing may pause for the insertion of thoughtful reflection.

Each Ladder is followed by a larger portion of the text in which it is found, a brief colloquy, and a collection of her more familiar sayings. The text is my own contemporary translation, found in A Revelation of Love, published in 2014.

Walter William Melnyk
The Transfiguration of Our Lord, 2014

Julian's Ladders

Julian of Norwich

Simple Ladders of Perfection

I. Three Spiritual Wounds
Julian's First Ladder
(Chapter 2)

Willful Longing for God

Natural Compassion

True Contrition

The First Ladder Passage

(Chapter 2)

These two desires, of the Passion and of the sickness, I desired with a condition, saying thus:

"Lord, You know what I want to have, but only if it is your will that I have it. If it be not your will, good Lord, be not displeased, for I desire nothing but your will."

For the third gift, by the grace of God and the teaching of Holy Church, I conceived a mighty desire to receive three wounds in my life; that is to say, the wound of true contrition, the wound of natural compassion, and the wound of a willful longing for God.

I asked this third petition without any conditions. The first two desires passed from my mind, but the third dwelt with me continually.

First Ladder Colloquy

Contrition, Compassion, Longing

In the "short text" of her book Julian tells us why she was moved to ask for "three wounds" as a gift from God:

"I heard a man of Holy Church tell the story of St. Cecelia, and from his explanation I understood that she received three wounds in the neck from a sword, through which she suffered death. Moved by this, I had a great desire, and prayed our Lord God that he would grant me in the course of my life three wounds, that is: the wound of contrition, the wound of compassion, and the wound of longing with all my will for God." (Showings, Colledge and Walsh, Paulist Press 1978, p, 127)

In the "long text," Julian enlarges upon her request, desiring *true* contrition and *natural* compassion.

We sometimes speak of a radically life-changing experience as a "wound." It is something that ends who we had been, and is healed in a way that makes us a different person. In the same way, we talk about being "wounded by love," perhaps recalling the arrows of Cupid. Julian desired her three wounds that she might, like St. Cecelia, be changed into a deeper lover of God.

Through her use of the Daily Office, Julian would have immersed herself in the psalms. They would have been a framework for her spirituality.

"A broken and contrite heart, O God, you will not despise." (Ps 51)

True contrition follows from an honest self-examination, in humility seeing ourselves as we truly are, neither ignoring our sins nor dwelling overmuch upon them. Seeing ourselves as we truly are before God frees us from the burdens of pretense and pride, enabling us to begin our spiritual ascent. It also frees us from the burden of constant self-absorption, that we may turn our concern outward toward others.

What is contrition within ourselves becomes, when we look toward others, compassion. Once we are no longer self-centered, we are able to see the burdens and trials of others, and to have compassion for them. Julian asked for a natural compassion for Christ in His suffering; a compassion at which she would not have to labor, but which would be "second nature" to her. Such compassion is to love Christ for His own sake, and not for what He can do for us. At the same time it enables us to have compassion in this natural world for all others. Honest self-understanding and unselfish compassion are the first two steps on this ladder.

Then we find, when we have gotten this far, that an intentional longing for God wells up in our own heart. We are changed from a self-centered person who loves God, to a lover of God who longs only for Him.

True Contrition

Natural Compassion

A Willful Longing for God

Julian Speaks

This creature had desired beforehand three gifts from God: The first was an understanding of His Passion; the second was a bodily sickness in youth, at thirty years of age; the third was to have, of God's gift, three wounds. (2)

For the Trinity is God; God is the Trinity. (4)

The Trinity is our maker and keeper, the Trinity is our everlasting lover, (4)

Where Jesus is, there the Trinity is understood. (4)

> "God, of your goodness, give me yourself,
> for you are enough to me,
> and I may ask for nothing that is less
> that may be full worship to you.
> And if I ask for anything less
> I shall always be in want,
> but only in you have I all." (5)

He is true endlessness (5)

Everything is just a part of His goodness, and there is nothing lacking in that. (6)

The goodness of God is the highest prayer, and it descends to the lowest level of our need. (6)

He does not despise that which He has made (6)

As the body is clad in cloth, and the flesh in the skin, and the bones in the flesh, and the heart in the breast, so are we, soul and body, clad in the goodness of God and there enclosed. (6)

Our natural will is to have God, and the good will of God is to have us. (6)

Our God and Lord, who is so holy and so awesome, is so homely and so courteous. (7)

Our whole life is grounded in faith, hope, and love. (7)

God is everything that is good, as I see it, and the goodness inherent in all things is God. (7)

I am not good because I have received a revelation, but only if it makes me love God better. (9)

In man is God, and God is in all. (9)

> By contrition we are made clean;
> by compassion we are made ready;
> by true longing for God we are made worthy. (39)

Julian of Norwich

Simple Ladders of Perfection

II. Seeking and Beholding
Julian's Second Ladder
(Chapter 10)

Trust Mightily

Wait Steadfastly

Seek Intentionally

Second Ladder Passage
(Chapter 10)

Now it is God's will that we have three things in our seeking: The first is that, without laziness, we seek as intentionally and energetically as we can through His grace, gladly and merrily, without useless despair or undue sorrow; The second is that we wait upon Him steadfastly for His love, without grumbling or rebelling against Him, until our life's end – for it shall last only a little while; The third is that we trust in Him mightily in fullness of faith, for this is His will. We know He shall appear suddenly and blissfully to all who love Him, for His working is secret, but He wants to be seen. His appearing shall be swift and sudden; and He wishes us to trust Him in this, for He is most courteous, and most homely, blessed may He be!

Second Ladder Colloquy

Seek, Wait, Trust

The delight of serendipity aside, we are much more likely to find something if we are looking for it. Perhaps God is not hard to find, but He may seem that way when we are not used to looking for Him. Indeed, when we first begin a search for God we do not know where to look, nor, perhaps, even what it is for which we are looking. The beginning of a search for God can be confusing, frustrating, daunting. The only way to avoid the "useless despair or undue sorrow" that initial failures can produce is to understand the only successful search for God takes place within the context of Grace.

Grace can be seen as the unasked-for presence of God. Julian reminds us it is unlikely that anyone has ever sought God without God having first revealed Himself to that person. Grace is prevenient: God comes to us before we ask. Seeking for God is not so much looking for Him "out there" as it is looking for Him within ourselves, where He already dwells. It is a place where we are not used to searching. So even if we believe the finding to be easy, the search itself can be difficult. It must be carried out "as intentionally and energetically as we can."

The second step on this ladder is a patient waiting; not the static waiting of inaction, but the dynamic waiting for the illusive results of an energetic search. This is the realization that no matter how diligently we seek, our seeking alone will never find Him. At least not in the way we might imagine. Otherwise we soon engage in grumbling and rebelling over such a difficult task. Only when we are prepared to acknowledge the search may take a lifetime are we able to perceive His sudden appearing.

So in the same action we seek and we await. To paraphrase Julian, "I sought Him, and I waited for Him." The path to God is always a Divine Paradox.

If we are willing to dwell in this Divine Paradox, seeking and waiting, we are gifted with the third step, a faithful trust. Not a trust in the coming of a resolution to the Paradox, but a trust that God is present within the Paradox, that seeking is indeed as good as beholding. The Beatific Vision does not appear at the end of the journey. The journey is the Beatific Vision.

Seek Intentionally

Wait Steadfastly

Trust Mightily

Julian Speaks

I saw Him, and I sought Him; I had Him, and I lacked Him. (10)

If a man or a woman were under the broad water, and should still have sight of God, for God is with a man continually, he should be safe in body and soul and suffer no harm. (10)

He wishes to be seen, and He wishes to be sought; He wishes to be waited for, and He wishes to be trusted. (10)

The soul is able to do no more than seek, suffer, and trust. (10)

Seeking is as good as beholding (10)

His appearing shall be swift and sudden; (10)

Julian of Norwich

Simple Ladders of Perfection

III. Three Degrees of Bliss
Julian's Third Ladder
(Chapter 14)

Eternal Bliss

Communal Bliss

Personal Bliss

The Third Ladder Passage
(Chapter 14)

And God showed three degrees of bliss that every soul shall have in heaven who has willfully served God in any degree here on earth.

The first is the honorable thanks he shall receive from our Lord God when he is finally delivered from all his earthly pain – thanks that is so high and so honorable he thinks it is enough all by itself. For I thought that all the pain and trouble that might be suffered by all living persons could not deserve the amount of honorable thanks that just one person will receive who has willfully served God.

The second degree of bliss is that all the blessed creatures who are in heaven shall witness this honorable thanking, and his service will be made known to them all. I saw this example: I king gives great honor to his servant by thanking him. But if the king makes this known to all the realm, then this honor is greatly increased.

The third is that as new and enjoyable as that honor is when first received, so it shall be forever.

Third Ladder Colloquy

Personal, Communal, Eternal

There are few things more pleasurable to the human soul than to be genuinely and sincerely thanked for one's efforts; to received evidence of being valued and appreciated. This is even more so when the thanks comes from one whom we love and honor. And yet more so when we know the thanks to be unmerited, that it comes from the love the other person has for us much more than from the value of what we have done.

So it is with God, who has no need of whatever we may do for Him, but nevertheless thanks us sincerely out of His love. He thanks us for the doing of it, even though it is He who has done it.

The first step is the bliss of experiencing God's thanks within our own heart. The next step is the bliss of an expanded heart: a heart that discovers itself to be in communion with all the saints. The bliss of God can no longer be contained within our own heart, for bliss shared is bliss multiplied, and bliss multiplied must be shared.

The final step is from the communal to the eternal. We are gifted with the realization that as God's thankfulness had no beginning, so it can have no ending.

The experience of Divine Bliss expands the heart from one alone, to one in many, to many in God.

Individual Bliss
Communal Bliss
Eternal Bliss

Julian Speaks

I saw God in a point (11)

There is no Doer but He (11)

> "See, I am God.
> See, I am in all things.
> See, I do all things.
> See, I never lift my hand from my works,
> nor ever shall, forever.
> See, I lead all things to the end I ordained for it,
> from without beginning, by the same might,
> wisdom, and love with which I made it.
> So how should anything be amiss?" (11)

The dearworthy blood of our Lord Jesus Christ, as truly as it is most precious, so truly is it most plentiful. (12)

There can be no wrath in God (12)

He keeps us equally safe, whether we are in woe or well. (15)

Bliss lasts eternally, while pain is passing (15)

I chose Jesus as my heaven (19)

It is a joy, a bliss, an endless liking to me that ever I suffered my Passion for You. And if I could suffer more, I would suffer more." (21)

Simple Ladders of Perfection

IV. Our Lady St. Mary
Julian's Fourth Ladder
(Chapter 25)

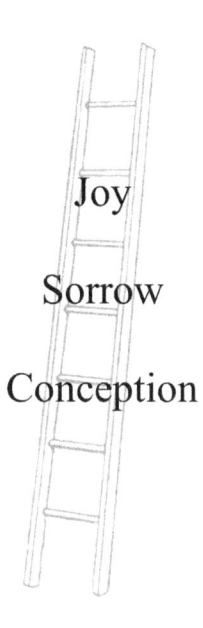

Joy

Sorrow

Conception

The Fourth Ladder Passage
(Chapter 25)

And for further understanding He showed me this example: If a man loves a creature uniquely above all other creatures, He will make all those creatures to love and delight in the one creature he loves so greatly. So in this word that Jesus said, "Will you see her?" I thought it was the most delightful thing He might have said to me about her, in this spiritual showing He gave me of her. And our Lord showed me nothing in such a special way except our lady Saint Mary, and He showed her three times: the first was as she conceived, the second was as she was in her sorrows under the cross, the third is as she is now, in delight, honor, and joy.

Fourth Ladder Colloquy

Conception, Sorrow, Joy

The wonder of conception, the sorrow of trials, the joy of fulfillment. Julian saw all these in her three visions of Our Lady Saint Mary: the wonder of youth in which she conceived her son, the sorrow and grief of a mother who watches her grown son die, the heavenly joy of fulfillment in her reign with Him in heaven. And this is Julian's fourth Ladder of Perfection.

It does not come as a surprise that the progression of motherhood is a powerful metaphor for the spiritual ascent. First the child is conceived in the womb, then come the trials and tribulations of growing up and making her way in the world, and finally the success of achievement in which the good parent participates vicariously, at a distance but still present in love.

So, too, our journey of the spirit begins when Christ appears within us. Like Mary, we have little to do with that except to say "Yes!" to God.

Then comes the struggle, often the pain, of ascent, for life is filled with the sorrows of tribulation, set-backs, down slides and dead ends.

But if we faithfully and courageously bear these trials with Christ, through His Passion and our own, at the end we will with

Him bear in endless joy a crown of glory. For, indeed, we are His glory, and we are His crown.

Conception

Sorrow

Joy

Julian Speaks

We are His bliss, we are His blessing, we are His worship, we are His crown (22)

He said sweetly, "If I could suffer more, I would suffer more." He did not say, "I it were necessary to suffer more," for even if it were not necessary, if He could suffer more, He would. (22)

"If you are satisfied, then I am satisfied." (23)

"Lo, how I loved you." (24)

Our Lord Jesus often said:
> I it am, I it am;
>
> I it am that is highest;
>
> I it am that you love;
>
> I it am that you enjoy;
>
> I it am that you serve;
>
> I it am for whom you long;
>
> I it am that you desire;
>
> I it am that you mean;
>
> I it am that is all;
>
> I it am that Holy Church preaches and teaches you;
>
> I it am that showed me here to you." (26)

All shall be well, and all shall be well, and all manner of thing shall be well." (26)

I did not see sin, for I believe it has no manner of substance, or any part of being. (27)

"It is true that sin is the cause of all this pain, but all shall be well, and all shall be well, and all manner of thing shall be well." These words were spoken quite tenderly, showing no manner of blame to me, or to any who shall be saved. (27)

I shall gather you up and put you back together, and make you gentle and humble, pure and holy, by making you one with me." (28)

> I may make all things well;
> I can make all things well;
> I will make all things well;
> I shall make all things well;
> and you shall see for yourself
> that all manner of thing shall be well. (31)

As truly as there is mercy and pity in God, so truly is there thirst and longing in Him. (31)

Simple Ladders of Perfection

There is a Deed that the blissful Trinity shall do on the last day, (32)

Just as the blessed Trinity made all things out of nothing, even so the same blessed Trinity shall make all well that is not well. (32)

What is impossible to you is not impossible to me. (32)

Julian of Norwich

V. About Our Praying
Julian's Fifth Ladder
(Chapter 42)

Union with God

Willful Prayer to God

Grounded in God

The Fifth Ladder Passage
(Chapter 42)

Our Lord wants us to have a true understanding of three things, in particular, relating to our prayers.

The first is to whom, and how, our prayers spring forth. By "to whom" He shows when He says, "I am ground." And "how," is by His goodness, for He says, "First it is my will."

For the second: in what manner and how we should use our prayers. It is so that our will be turned to the will of our Lord, rejoicing. Thus His meaning when He says, "I make you to will it."

For the third: that we know the fruit and the result of our prayers. That is, to be come as one with our Lord, and like Him, in all things. And to convey this meaning, and for this end, was all this lovely lesson shown; and He shall help us, and we shall do it, just as He said – blessed may He be!

Fifth Ladder Colloquy

Ground, Prayer, Union

Archimedes is reputed to have said, "Give me a lever long enough and a fulcrum on which to place it, and I shall move the world."

He knew that before he could do anything, he needed a place to stand, solid ground upon which to place his fulcrum. And upon the unmoving, grounded fulcrum, he would need the action of a great lever. Given those two things, he could accomplish anything. He could move the world.

So, too, with our own Ladder of Perfection. We need the stability of unmoving groundedness upon which to place our ladder. That stability is God, who is the Ground of our Being, and so the Ground of our Prayer. God is dependable for our prayers, for He is the creator of our Prayer. Not just the subject of our prayers, but the being of Prayer itself. "First I do it," He told Julian, "then I cause you to wish it, and then I cause you to pray for it. How then shall it be that you shall not have it?" Understand this: it is this dependable, unmoving groundedness that is for us the Goodness of God. God is the fulcrum, and the ground upon which it stands.

And God is the lever which we use, the Prayer that wells up within us. For Prayer is not the words we use to ask God to do things. Prayer, true Prayer, is the Presence of God within the soul. And He is the author of that will with which we welcome that presence.

First we experience our groundedness in God. Then we willfully immerse ourselves in Prayer, which is the practicing of His presence.

Finally we experience the result, the fruit of this prayer. It is not to receive things, or to cause things to happen. Clement of Alexandria wrote in the second century that the spiritual person prays not to have good things added to him, but that he, himself, might be good. The desired and true Fruit of Prayer is union with God. First God knits us to Himself. Then He causes us to desire it, and then He causes us to prayer for it. How shall it then be that we shall not have this union with Himself?

In Julian's wonderful idiom, "Prayer oneth the soul to God."

Ground
Prayer
Union

Julian Speaks

The fullness of joy is to behold God in all things (35)

By His allowing we fall; in His blissful love with His might and His wisdom we are preserved; by mercy and grace we are raised to manifold joys. (35)

My sin shall not stop His goodness from working. (36)

"I keep you completely safe." (37)

In every soul that shall be saved is a Godly will that never assented to sin and never shall (37)

God considers sin as a sorrow and a pain to those who love Him, and because He loves them, he assigns them no blame. (39)

Peace and love are always in us, abiding and working, but we are not always in peace and love. (39)

It is a supreme friendship of our courteous Lord that He protects us so tenderly while we are in sin. (40)

He ever longs to bring us into the fullness of joy, (40)

As mighty and wise God is to save man, just so is He willing. (40)

Often we are as barren and dry after our prayers as we were before. In our folly, this feeling is a cause of weakness in us. I know, because I have felt it in myself. (41)

"I am the ground of your praying:
first it is my will that you have it,
and then I make you to want it,
and then I make you pray for it;
and you do pray for it.
how should it then be that you should not receive
what you pray for?" (41)

It is most impossible that we should ask for mercy and grace and not have it; (41)

Praying is a fresh, gracious and enduring will of the soul, made one with and fastened into the will of our Lord by the sweet and secret working of the Holy Spirit. (41)

Full glad and merry is our Lord because of our prayer. (41)

Pray inwardly, even if you think it gives you no pleasure. It is beneficial even though you feel nothing. (41)

All of your living is prayer in my sight." (41)

VI. To Pray is to Follow Jesus
Julian's Sixth Ladder
(Chapter 43)

Drawn into Jesus

Led By Jesus

Followed by Jesus

The Sixth Ladder Passage
(Chapter 43)

I well understand that the more the soul sees of God, the more it desires Him, by His grace. But when we do not see Him we feel a reason and desire to pray, because of our failings, confessing ourselves to Jesus. For when the soul is tempest-tossed, troubled, and left to himself in turmoil, then it is time to pray to make himself pliable and obedient to God. But the soul, by no manner of prayer, can make God pliant to him, for God is always the same in love.

I learned that when we see needs that we pray for, then our good Lord follows us, assisting our desire. And when we, through His special grace, see Him clearly, seeing no other needs but Him, then we follow after Him and He draws us into Himself in love. For I saw and felt that His marvelous and fulsome goodness completes our abilities.

Sixth Ladder Colloquy

Jesus Follows Us, We Follow Jesus, Jesus Enfolds Us

When we first begin to pray, we do not understand the purpose of prayer. Initially this is because we are children bodily, and have not yet been taught a deeper understanding of the Faith. (With St. Paul we say, "When I was a child, I spoke like a child, I thought like a child, I reasoned like a child." (I Corinthians 13) When we first begin to pray, we ask for things, as if they were of greatest importance: to receive this thing, to avoid that, to cause or prevent the happening of some other thing. Sometimes we receive what we ask for, sometimes not, and we do not understand we would have received or not received the same anyway, even if we had not prayed. Know this: prayer does not change God's mind. Prayer does not teach God that we know of a better way than His. When it comes to things, we always think in terms of "better," but God only thinks in terms of "Best." How could we, by prayer, convince God to give us something better than the Best He has already planned? "The soul, by no manner of prayer, can make God pliant to him, for God is always the same in love."

So all the while we are on the first step of this Ladder, earnestly praying, but misunderstanding prayer, Jesus follows along behind us, watching us, like a shepherd follows his flock. From this protective position He will not allow harm to come to us, and He will call out to us as a shepherd calls to His sheep, suggesting our next move, guiding our growth in prayer though we know it not. He assists us in our desire, until we desire only Him. For he is enough.

The second step is when we see Him clearly, and realize we have no other need but only Him. "God, of your goodness give me yourself, for you are enough to me, and I can ask for nothing less that will truly honor you. If I ask for anything that is less I shall always be in want, for only in you have I all."

In this second step Jesus no longer follows along behind us, for we have learned to follow Him.

The third step naturally proceeds from this. When we realize He is enough, we find ourselves drawn in to Him and we experience the purpose of prayer: the uniting of the soul with God. Then we only pray according to His will, and His will is only that we be one with Him.

Jesus Follows Us

Jesus Leads Us

Jesus Enfolds Us

Julian Speaks

No one asks for mercy and grace, truly meaning it, except that mercy and grace have already been given to him. (42)

Sometimes we think we have prayed for a long time, and yet, we think, we have not received what we have been asking for. But we should not despair in this. For I am certain, as I understand our Lord, that either we await a better time, or more grace, or a better gift. (42)

Prayer is a rightful understanding of the fullness of joy that is to come, with a good longing and a sure trust. (42)

Prayer unites us with God (43)

The soul, by prayer, accords with the will of God. (43)

All the reasons we pray are wrapped up into seeing and contemplating Him, to whom we pray, (43)

God is always the same in love. (43)

Julian of Norwich

VII. Like the Trinity
Julian's Seventh Ladder
(Chapter 44)

Delight in God (Love)

Contemplate God (Wisdom)

Perceive God (Truth)

The Seventh Ladder Passage
(Chapter 44)

Truth sees God, and wisdom contemplates God. And out of these two comes a third: a holy and marvelous delight in God, which is love. Where truth and wisdom are truly found, there is love truly found, in common with them both, and all three of God's making. For He is eternal, almighty Truth, eternal almighty Wisdom, and eternal almighty Love, all uncreated. And man's soul is a creature of God, yet has the same properties as God, yet is created. And forever the soul does what it was made for: it sees God, it contemplates God, and it loves God. In this, God rejoices in the creature, and the creature rejoices in God, eternally marveling. In this marveling he sees his God, his Lord, his Maker, so high, so great, and so good compared to the creature who is made, that the creature almost seems to himself to be nothing. But clarity and purity of truth and wisdom make him to know and understand that he has been made for love, in which God protects him forever.

Seventh Ladder Colloquy

Truth, Wisdom, Love

One of the great questions in the Gospel stories was asked by the Roman Prefect of Judea, Pontius Pilate:

"What is truth?"

St. John records the question, but not the answer, because he is not telling Pilate's story, but the story of Jesus. One must assume it was a question that would have impressed and moved Jesus under other circumstances. Was it rhetorical; another way of saying there is no such thing as truth? Was it an attempt to find a way out of the judgment he was being maneuvered into making? Was it a genuine search for understanding? We will never know.

But we do know this clearly: Seeking the truth is the first step along the road to wisdom. The light of truth frees us from the darkness of ignorance. The Psalmist tells us God's True Word "is a lamp unto my feet." (Psalm 119:105) And it is by the Lamp of Truth that we can see; can see God.

The first step in this Ladder of Perfection is to seek the Truth, by which we may be able to see God.

As we contemplate what we have seen, we come to know God, to obtain Divine Wisdom. The purity of Truth and the Clarity of Wisdom bring us to the third step, to Delight in the unmediated experience of Divine Love.

By Truth we see; through Wisdom we contemplate; in Love we find delight.

Truth

Wisdom

Love

Julian Speaks

He is eternal, almighty Truth, eternal almighty Wisdom, and eternal almighty Love, all uncreated. (44)

I saw most truly that our Lord was never wrathful, and never shall be, for He is God (46)

God is the goodness that may not be wrathful, for He is nothing but goodness. (46)

I saw no wrath, except on man's part, and He forgives that in us; (48)

The ground of mercy is love, and the working of mercy is our preservation in love. (48)

Our Lord God, as regards Himself, may not forgive, for He may not be angry – it is not possible (49)

I saw full surely that where our Lord appears, peace comes, and wrath has no place. (49)

I saw no manner of wrath in God, (49)

We are securely safe by the merciful protection of God, so that we may not perish. (49)

God is our very peace, and He is our sure keeper when we ourselves are not peaceful; (49)

I saw our Lord God showing toward us no more blame than as if we were pure and holy as the angels are in heaven. (50)

The Parable of the Lord and the Servant (51)

In the eyes of God, all men are one man, and one man is all men. (51)

When Adam fell, God's Son fell. Because of the true union that was made in heaven, God's Son could not be separated from Adam, and by Adam I understood all men. Adam fell from life to death, into the bog of this wretched world, and after that into hell. God's Son fell with Adam into the bog of the maiden's womb, who was the fairest daughter of Adam, in order to excuse Adam from blame in all heaven and earth; and mightily He fetched him out of hell. (51)

Our Father may – nay, will – assign no more blame to us than to His own Son, dearworthy Christ. (51)

Jesus is all that shall be saved, and all that shall be saved is Jesus. (51)

I saw that God rejoices that He is our Father,
    God rejoices that He is our Mother,
    and God rejoices that He is our true Spouse,
    and our soul is His beloved wife;
    and Christ rejoices that He is our Brother,
    and Jesus rejoices that He is our Savior. (52)

He wishes us to trust that He is with us always, and in three ways: First He is with us in heaven, as true man in His own person drawing us up, and that was shown in His spiritual thirst;
And He is with us and leading us here on earth, and that was shown in the third showing, where I saw God in a point; And He is with us in our soul, endlessly dwelling there, ruling us and caring for us, (52)

God's sight is one thing, and man's sight is another. It is man's nature humbly to accuse himself, and it is the nature of God's goodness courteously to excuse man. (52)

In every soul that shall be saved is a godly will which has never assented to sin, nor ever shall (53)

I saw that God never began to love mankind; for just exactly as mankind shall be in endless bliss fulfilling the joy of God regarding His works, so too the same mankind has been, in the foresight of God, known and loved from without beginning. (53)

Before God made us, He loved us. (53)

Thus is man's soul made by God, and in the same time knit to God. (53)

There may, nor shall, be absolutely nothing between God and man's soul. (53)

Because of the great and endless love that God has for all mankind, He makes no distinction between the blessed soul of Christ and the least soul that shall be saved. (54)

Our soul is meant to be God's dwelling-place, and the dwelling-place of the soul is God, (54)

God our maker dwells in our soul. (54)

I saw no difference between God and our own essence, but it was as if it were all God. (54)

We are enclosed in Him, and He in us (54)

Faith is nothing else but a right understanding with a true belief and a secure trust of our very being that we are in God, and God is in us, even if we cannot see it. (54)

We live more truly in heaven than on earth. (54)

I saw with complete certainty that our essence is in God, and I also saw that God is in our fleshliness. (55)

Our soul is a created Trinity, like the uncreated blissful Trinity, (55)

God is nearer to us than our own soul; for He is the ground upon whom our soul stands (56)

We may not come to know our soul until we first have a knowing of God, (56)

His natural Godhead causes mercy and grace to be at work in us, and the natural Godhead we have from Him enables us to receive the working of mercy and grace. (57)

For love He made mankind, and for the same love He himself would be man. (57)

Our Savior is our true Mother, in whom we shall be endlessly born, yet shall never come out from Him. (57)

> God almighty is our natural Father,
> and God all wisdom is our natural Mother,
> with the love and the goodness of the Holy Spirit;

all one God, one Lord.

And in the knitting and the uniting,

    He is our very true Spouse,

    and we are His beloved wife and His fair maiden, (58)

Simple Ladders of Perfection

VIII. Becoming Like God
Julian's Eighth Ladder
(Chapter 58)

Deification

Sanctification

Creation

The Eighth Ladder Passage
(Chapter 58)

For our whole life is experienced in three stages: in the first we have our being, and in the second we have our increasing, and in the third we have our fulfilling. The first is nature, the second is mercy, and the third is grace.

As regards the first, I saw and understood that:

the high might of the Trinity is our Father,

and the deep wisdom of the Trinity is our Mother,

and the great love of the Trinity is our Lord;

and all this we have in nature, and in our essential making. Furthermore, I saw in the Second Person, who is our Mother in essence, that same dearworthy Person has become our Mother in our flesh.

Eighth Ladder Colloquy
Creation, Sanctification, Deification

In the Eighth Ladder we see most clearly the influence of Eastern Christianity upon Julian's thought. Anglican liturgy is Western; decidedly Roman in quality. But Anglican spirituality is Eastern; brought from the Eastern Churches by John Cassian in the early fifth century CE.

Western Christianity, overwhelmed by wars and plagues in its first thousand years, developed a spirituality based upon the wickedness of man and the brokenness of man's relationship with God. We are created good, they affirmed, but evidence shows we always fall into sin. Therefore we must be judged, and through Divine Judgment God brings us to redemption. At its base, Western Spirituality has a four-step Ladder of Perfection:

Creation, Sin, Judgment, Redemption

The Eastern Church, where the idea of the Trinity was developed by the Cappadocian Fathers and ratified at the Council of Nicea in the early fourth century CE, was during that time less troubled by manmade and natural disasters, and developed a more optimistic three-fold (Trinitarian?) Spirituality. They, too, affirmed we are created good by God. But then throughout our journey of faith the Holy Spirit works upon us constantly to make us more holy, more sanctified. Finally, in heaven, we are assumed into the Trinity and deified, or made like God:

Creation, Sanctification, Deification

Because the soul is knit to God in creation, there is never a time when we are not reaching for heaven. Julian's Eighth Ladder begins with our Creation. And not just our birth, or our conception, but our Creation in the mind of God before worldly Creation took shape or form. Because you are a Creature, you have already stepped upon the Ladder of Perfection.

Our entire life is the second step of the ascent. Day after day, year after year, in all that happens to us and in all that we think, say or do in return, the Holy Spirit acts upon us to increase us in holiness.

All is in preparation for the final step, being drawn into the Godhead in eternal Bliss and made one with God. Not just tied to God, or wed to God, or made an important part of God; to *be* God, along with God's self. (If you find this last a stumbling block, it is likely because you are a product of the Western Church.)

Creation

Sanctification

Deification

Julian Speaks

As truly as God is our Father, so truly God is our Mother. (59)

He said:
> "I it Am," which is to say
> "I it Am: the might and goodness of the Fatherhood.
> I it Am: the wisdom of the Motherhood.
> I it Am: the light and the grace that is all blessed love.
> I it Am: the Trinity.
> I it Am: the Unity.
> I Am the sovereign goodness of all manner of things.
> I Am that which causes you to love.
> I Am that which causes you to yearn.
> I it Am: the endless fulfilling of all true desires. (59)

The soul is highest, noblest, and worthiest when it is lowest, humblest, and gentlest (59)

We know that all our mothers only bear us to pain and death. But our true Mother, Jesus, who is all love, bears us to joy and to eternal life, blessed may He be! (60)

A mother may lay her child tenderly *upon* her breast, but our tender Mother Jesus, He may homely lead us *into* His blessed breast through His sweet open side, (60)

He kindles our understanding, He guides our ways, He eases our conscience, He comforts our soul, He lightens our heart. (61)

God is nature in His very being; that is to say, all goodness in nature is God. He is the ground, the essence, the same thing as nature; He is the true Father and the true Mother of nature. (62)

Nature and grace are of one accord; for grace is from God just as nature is from God. (63)

He enlivened us by taking our nature upon Himself, and in His blessed dying upon the cross He birthed us into eternal life. (63)

"You shall suddenly be taken up from all pain, from all your sickness, from all your distress, and from all your woe. And you shall come up above, and you shall have me for your reward, and you shall be fulfilled in love and in bliss. (64)

It is more blissful that a man be taken from pain, than for pain to be taken from a man; for if pain is taken from us, it may come back again. (64)

Jesus will never leave this place that He takes in our soul, for in us is His homeliest home, and His endless dwelling. (67)

He did not say, "You shall not be tempest-tossed," but He said "You shall not be overcome." (68)

Julian of Norwich

IX. Three Faces of Christ
Julian's Ninth Ladder
(Chapter 71)

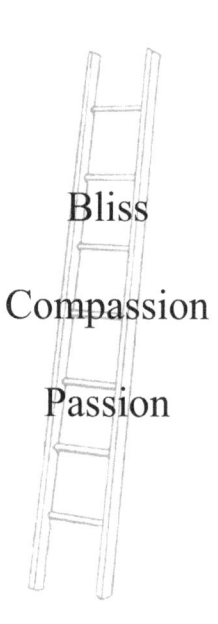

Bliss

Compassion

Passion

The Ninth Ladder Passage
(Chapter 71)

Glad and merry and sweet is the blissful and lovely face our Lord shows to our souls. For He beholds us always living in love-longing for Him. So He wills that our soul be of glad countenance towards Him, to give Him the same reward. Thus I hope that by His grace He has – and shall even more – influence our inner purpose by our outward expression, and make us all one with Him and with one another, in Jesus, our true lasting joy.

I understood three kinds of expressions from our Lord. The first is the face of His Passion, as He showed it while He was here in this life and death. Though this sight is mournful and sorrowful, so is it glad and merry, for He is God. The second manner of expression is pity, and sympathy, and compassion; He shows this in certain protection to His lovers who hold to His mercy. The third is His blissful face as it shall be without end, and this expression appeared the most often for the longest time in the showings.

Ninth Ladder Colloquy

Passion, Compassion, Bliss

We have very nearly come full circle back to the First Ladder. While the two are not identical they complement each other closely.

In our journey through life – and His – Christ shows us three faces, by His grace, to care for the changing situations in which we find ourselves.

We are at first troubled by weakness and sin. So Christ's first face is that of His Passion. We think it mournful and suffering, Julian writes, but it is also glad and merry because it is God making amends for us. Mind of this passion inspires in us Contrition, the first step in growth.

As we grow, still having to deal with the dangers of the world and the weakness of our own hearts, He shows Pity and Compassion towards us; not judging or punishing us for sins borne of wickedness, but healing us and encouraging us for the injury that sins are. (God never forgives us, Julian insists, because he is never angry at us.) This sympathy and compassion of Christ encourages sympathy and compassion in our own hearts for others, and we take the second step on the Ladder. The final step is the same as with the Eighth Ladder: the Beatific Vision, union with God. It is significant with Mother Julian that not all her simple

Ladders of Perfection take place in this world in order to prepare us to move on to Heaven. Some of her Ladders actually bridge Earth and Heaven, beginning here and ending there. Thus, as the words of the Exsultet proclaim, are Heaven and Earth forever joined together.

Passion
Compassion
Bliss

Julian Speaks

Some of us believe that God is almighty and may do all,
and some believe that He is all wisdom and can do all,
but that He is all love and will do all, there we stop short. (71)

Just as God courteously forgives our sins when we repent, even so it is His will that we also forgive ourselves of sin: (73)

We shall in love be homely, and near to God; and we shall in dread be gentle and courteous to God; both alike equal. (74)

Whether it is that we are foul or pure, we are all one in His love (76)

We flee to our Lord and we shall be comforted; we touch Him and we shall be made pure; we cleave to Him and we shall be secure and safe from all manner of peril. (77)

The blessed comfort that I saw is large enough for us all. (79)

Julian of Norwich

Simple Ladders of Perfection

X. Turning to Jesus
Julian's Tenth Ladder
(Chapter 82)

Cleaving

Repenting

Sorrowing

The Tenth Ladder Passage
(Chapter 82)

And here I understood that our Lord beholds His servant with pity, and not with blame; for this passing life does not ask us to live completely without blame and sin. He loves us endlessly, and we sin habitually, and He shows this to us full tenderly; then we sorrow and mourn discreetly, turning ourselves to the beholding of His mercy, cleaving to His love and goodness, seeing that He is our remedy, knowing that we do nothing but sin. And this is the humility that we receive by beholding our sin. Faithfully we know His everlasting love; and thanking and praising Him, we please Him.

"I love you, and you love me; and our love shall never be separated in two, and it is for your benefit that I suffer."

Tenth Ladder Colloquy

Sorrowing, Repenting, Cleaving

We go through most of our adult Christian lives guided by the simplistic (and therefore often wrong) ideas we were taught in Sunday School. Most people think repenting is being sorry for our sins. The unfortunate, and usually unexamined, implication is that being sorry is enough. It is like the chronically disobedient child who is always saying "I'm sorry," but never changes.

The word "repent" means "turn around." Before we can turn around we must have a motivation for doing so, and that motivation is our sorrow for what we have become. The first step on this ladder is to be sorry. The second step is to change, to turn around and go the other way, to repent.

If you have read this far in Julian (and, it is hoped, have gone far beyond childhood Sunday School in your Christian Discipleship!) you will know that neither your sorrow nor your repenting will or can cause God to forgive you. God's grace is "prevenient." It "comes before" our turning to Him. God does not forgive you because you have repented in sorrow (indeed He never forgives you, He cannot, for He is never angry at you.) Here is how it works:

You realize sorrow and act to repent because God has already led you to do so. ("First I do it, then I cause you to want it, then I cause you to pray for it: can it then be you could not have it?") God is on both sides of this Divine equation. This is why Julian tells us "There is no Doer but He."

Even the final step, cleaving to God, is not something we do, but is His ultimate affirmation of us: God cleaves us to Himself.

Sorrowing

Repenting

Cleaving

Julian Speaks

Man is grounded in this life by three things; and by these three God is honored, and we are helped, protected, and saved.

> The first is by use of man's natural reason;
>
> The second is by the common teaching of Holy Church;
>
> The third is the inward gracious inspiration of the Holy Spirit.

These three are all of one God (80)

Love never allows itself to be without pity. (80)

He tenderly excuses us, and ever shields us from any blame in His sight. (80)

It is the most honor to Him of anything that we might do, that we live in our penance gladly and merrily because of His love; (81)

Our Lord beholds His servant with pity, and not with blame; (82)

"I love you, and you love me; and our love shall never be separated in two, (82)

In the sight of God we do not fall, and in our own sight we do not stand. Both of these are true, as I see it, but the way our Lord God sees it is the highest truth. (82)

And in the end all shall be love. (84)

And from the time that it was shown, I often desired to understand what was our Lord's meaning. And fifteen years after and more I was answered in this spiritual understanding:

"Would you know your Lord's meaning in this thing?

Know it well, love was His meaning.

Who showed it to you? Love.

What did He show you? Love.

Why did He show it? For love.

Keep yourself in that love, and you shall understand and know more in the same,

But you shall never know nor understand therein anything else, without end."

Thus was I taught that love was our Lord's meaning. (86)

In our making we had a beginning; but the love wherein He made us was in Him from without beginning; and it is in this love that we have our beginning. (86)

Julian Prayers

Collects for the Feast of Julian of Norwich
from the Book of Common Prayer

Lord God, in your compassion you granted to the Lady Julian many revelations of your nurturing and sustaining love: Move our hearts, like hers, to seek you above all things, for in giving us yourself you give us all; through Jesus Christ our Lord, who lives and reigns with you and the Holy Spirit, one God, for ever and ever. *Amen.*

from Common Worship, Church of England

Most holy God, the ground of our beseeching, who through your servant Julian revealed the wonders of your love: grant that as we are created in your nature and restored by your grace, our wills may be so made one with yours that we may come to see you face to face and gaze on you for ever; through Jesus Christ your Son our Lord, who is alive and reigns with you, in the unity of the Holy Spirit, one God, now and for ever.

A Prayer for the Order of Julian of Norwich

O Lord Jesus Christ, guide and sanctify us and our brothers and sisters whom you have called to follow you in poverty, chastity, obedience, and prayer in the spirit of Blessed Mother Julian; protect us from danger and want, and grant that by our prayer and service we may enrich your Church, and by our life and worship we may glorify your Name; for you reign with the Father and the Holy Spirit, one God, now and for ever. Amen.

The Prayer of Mother Julian
from A Revelation of Divine Love

God, of your goodness, give me yourself,
for you are enough to me,
and I may ask for nothing that is less
that may be full worship to you.
And if I ask anything that is less
I shall always be in want,
for only in you have I all.

The Julian Oblate

by Walter William Melnyk

Gift and gifted,
the Oblate lives
at the boundary of
offerings; gives
self to Christ,
receives Christ in return.
Giver and gifted,
the Oblate yearns
for Christ,
and for Christ lives,
yet lingers in the world
to tell
to straining hearts
the Promise that this
Christ imparts;
that all will be well,
and all manner of thing
will be well.

Simple Ladders of Perfection

Julian's Views of the Trinity

There is scarcely a page in Julian's book in which she does not dwell upon the love of the Trinity for humankind. So it is no surprise her many Ladders of Perfection, Ladders of Spiritual Ascent, all have three steps. Here are a few of her Trinitarian passage:

Chapter Four

In this same showing, suddenly the Trinity filled my heart full of joy. And I knew it will be this way for ever in heaven, to all those who shall come there.

For the Trinity is God; God is the Trinity. The Trinity is our maker and keeper, the Trinity is our everlasting lover, and our everlasting joy and bliss, in our Lord Jesus Christ. This was shown to me in the first revelation, and in all of them, for as I see it, where Jesus is, there the Trinity is understood.

Chapter Ten

We know by our faith, and the preaching and teaching of Holy Church, that the blessed Trinity made mankind in His own image and likeness. In the same way, we know that when man fell so deeply and so wretchedly because of sin, there was no other help to restore him except Him that created man. For He that made man for the sake of love, would by the same love restore man to bliss, even greater than before. And even as we were made in the likeness of the Trinity in our first making, our maker wishes that we should be like our savior Jesus Christ, in heaven without end, by virtue of our remaking. And between these two makings, He would, for love and honor toward man, make Himself as much like man in this mortal life – in our foulness and our wretchedness – as man might be without guilt.

Chapter Eleven

Nothing shall ever fail in this, for He made everything in complete goodness, and therefore the blessed Trinity is forever fully pleased with all His works.

All this He showed in complete bliss, meaning this:
"See, I am God.
See, I am in all things.
See, I do all things.
See, I never lift my hand from my works,
nor ever shall, forever.

Chapter Twenty-Three

Jesus wishes that we carefully behold the bliss over our salvation that is in the blissful Trinity, so that we may desire to have as much spiritual appreciation, with His grace, as described before. That is to say, that we enjoy our salvation just as much as Christ does, while we are here.

The whole Trinity was at work in the Passion of Christ, ministering to us an abundance of virtues and plentiful grace through Him. But it was only the maiden's son who suffered. And in this Passion the blessed Trinity endlessly rejoices.

Chapter Thirty-One

And so our good Lord answered all the questions and doubts I might make, fully comforting me in saying:
I may make all things well;
I can make all things well;
I will make all things well;
I shall make all things well;
and you shall see for yourself that all manner of thing shall be well.

That He said "I may," I understood for the Father; that He said, "I can," I understood for the Son; that He said "I will," I understood for the Holy Spirit; and where He said, "I shall," I understood for the unity of the blessed Trinity, three persons and one truth; and where He said "You shall see for Yourself," I understood the uniting of all mankind that shall be saved into the blissful Trinity.

Chapter Thirty-Two

There is a deed that the blissful Trinity shall do on the last day, as I see it. When that Deed shall be, and how it shall be done, is unknown to all creatures that are beneath Christ. And it shall be so until the time it is done. He wishes us to understand this so that we might be more at ease in our soul, in peace and love, leaving aside concern about all the tempests that might keep us from the truth, and from rejoicing in Him. This is the Great Deed ordained by our Lord God from without beginning, treasured and hidden in His blessed breast, known only to Himself. And by this Deed He shall indeed make all things well. For just as the blessed Trinity made all things out of nothing, even so the same blessed Trinity shall make all well that is not well.

Chapter Fifty-Three

I saw that God never began to love mankind; for just exactly as mankind shall be in endless bliss fulfilling the joy of God regarding His works, so too the same mankind has been, in the foresight of God, known and loved from without beginning, in accord with God's rightful intention.

And by the endless assent in full accord of the whole Trinity, the Mid-Person wished to be the foundation and head of this fair human nature, out of Whom we all come, in Whom we are all enclosed, into Whom we shall all wend our way; finding in Him our full heaven in everlasting joy, by the foreseeing purpose of all the blessed Trinity from without beginning.

For before God made us, He loved us.
And when we were made, we loved Him;

and this is a love made from the natural essential goodness of the Holy Spirit, mighty by reason of the might of the Father, and wise in mind of the wisdom of God the Son. Thus is man's soul made by God, and in the same time knit to God.

Chapter Fifty-Four

I saw that God never began to love mankind; for just exactly as mankind shall be in endless bliss fulfilling the joy of God regarding His works, so too the same mankind has been, in the foresight of God, known and loved from without beginning, in accord with God's rightful intention.

And by the endless assent in full accord of the whole Trinity, the Mid-Person wished to be the foundation and head of this fair human nature, out of Whom we all come, in Whom we are all enclosed, into Whom we shall all wend our way; finding in Him our full heaven in everlasting joy, by the foreseeing purpose of all the blessed Trinity from without beginning.

For before God made us, He loved us.

And when we were made, we loved Him;
and this is a love made from the natural essential goodness of the Holy Spirit, mighty by reason of the might of the Father, and wise in mind of the wisdom of God the Son. Thus is man's soul made by God, and in the same time knit to God.

Chapter Fifty-Five

Thus was my understanding led by God: to see in Him and understand, to learn and to know, that our soul is a created Trinity, like the uncreated blissful Trinity, and is known and loved from without beginning, being united to the Creator, as I have said before. This sight was very sweet and marvelous to behold, peaceful and restful, secure and delectable.

And because of the honorable union that was thus made by God between the soul and body, it is necessary that mankind should be restored from the double death of both body and soul. This restoration could never take place until such time as the Second Person of the Trinity had taken on the lower part of mankind, to which the higher part had been united in the original creation. And then these two parts of mankind were united in Christ, the higher and the lower, which make up one unified soul.

Chapter Fifty-Eight

God, the blissful Trinity, which is everlasting Being, as surely as He is endless from without beginning, even so it was in His endless purpose to create mankind, whose fair nature was first given to His own Son, the Second Person.

And when He wished, with full agreement with all the Trinity, He made us all at once; and when He made us, He knit and joined us to Himself. By this union we are preserved as pure and as noble as when we were made. By virtue of this same precious uniting, we love our maker and delight in Him, praising him, thanking Him, and endlessly rejoicing in Him. Such is the work which is wrought by God in every soul that shall be saved: the Godly will which I mentioned before. Thus in our making:

God almighty is our natural Father,
and God all wisdom is our natural Mother,
with the love and the goodness of the Holy Spirit;
all one God, one Lord.

I beheld the working of all the blessed Trinity, in which consideration I saw these three properties:

the property of the Fatherhood,
the property of the Motherhood,
and the property of Lordhood in one God.

And when He wished, with full agreement with all the Trinity, He made us all at once; and when He made us, He knit and joined us to Himself. By this union we are preserved as pure and as noble as when we were made. By virtue of this same precious

uniting, we love our maker and delight in Him, praising him, thanking Him, and endlessly rejoicing in Him. Such is the work which is wrought by God in every soul that shall be saved: the Godly will which I mentioned before. Thus in our making:
>God almighty is our natural Father,
>and God all wisdom is our natural Mother,
>with the love and the goodness of the Holy Spirit;
>all one God, one Lord.

For our whole life is experienced in three stages: in the first we have our being, and in the second we have our increasing, and in the third we have our fulfilling. The first is nature, the second is mercy, and the third is grace.
>As regards the first, I saw and understood that:
>the high might of the Trinity is our Father,
>and the deep wisdom of the Trinity is our Mother,
>and the great love of the Trinity is our Lord;

and all this we have in nature, and in our essential making.

Chapter Fifty-Nine

As truly as God is our Father, so truly God is our Mother. He showed this in all the showings, but especially in these sweet words, where He said:
>"I it Am," which is to say
>"I it Am: the might and goodness of the Fatherhood.
>I it Am: the wisdom of the Motherhood.
>I it Am: the light and the grace that is all blessed love.
>I it Am: the Trinity.
>I it Am: the Unity.
>I Am the sovereign goodness of all manner of things.
>I Am that which causes you to love.
>I Am that which causes you to yearn.
>I it Am: the endless fulfilling of all true desires.

Chapter Seventy-One

I understood three kinds of expressions from our Lord. The first is the face of His Passion, as He showed it while He was here in this life and death. Though this sight is mournful and sorrowful, so is it glad and merry, for He is God. The second manner of expression is pity, and sympathy, and compassion; He shows this in certain protection to His lovers who hold to His mercy. The third is His blissful face as it shall be without end, and this expression appeared the most often for the longest time in the showings.

Thus in the time of our pain and our woe, He shows us the face of His Passion and of His cross, helping us to endure better, with His own blessed strength. And in the time of our sinning, He shows us the face of compassion and pity, protecting and defending us mightily against all our enemies. And these first two are the ordinary faces He shows to us in this life.

Mingled with these two is the third, and that is His blessed face, a bit like it shall be in heaven. That is a gracious blessing and sweet illuminating of the spiritual life, by which we are preserved in certain faith, hope and love, with contrition and devotion, with contemplation and with all manner of true solace and sweet comforts. The blissful face of our Lord God produces this in us by grace.

Chapter Seventy-Three

Though the three Persons of the Trinity are all equal in themselves, the soul received most understanding in love. Yes, and in all things He wills that we have our beholding and rejoicing in love. And yet of this knowing we are most blind.
> For some of us believe that God is almighty and may do all,
> and some believe that He is all wisdom and can do all,
> but that He is all love and will do all, there we stop short.

Chapter Seventy-Five

I saw three kinds of longing in God, all with the same purpose; and we have the same in us in the same strength, for the same end.

The first is that He longs to teach us to know Him and love Him evermore, because that is beneficial and helpful to us.

The second is that He longs to have us come up into His bliss, as souls are when they taken out of pain into heaven.

The third is to complete us in bliss, and that shall be on the last day, and shall last forever. For I saw, as it is known in our faith, that pain and sorrow shall come to an end for all who shall be saved.

Chapter Eighty-Six

And from the time that it was shown, I often desired to understand what was our Lord's meaning. And fifteen years after and more I was answered in this spiritual understanding:

"Would you know your Lord's meaning in this thing?

Know it well, love was His meaning.

Who showed it to you? Love.

What did He show you? Love.

Why did He show it? For love.

Keep yourself in that love, and you shall understand and know more in the same,

But you shall never know nor understand therein anything else, without end."

Thus was I taught that love was our Lord's meaning.

Also from Walter William Melnyk:

A Revelation of Divine Love
Julian of Norwich
Hazelnut Press, 2014
ISBN13: 978-1499123982
ISBN10: 1499123981

This work began as a personal Lenten devotional discipline. It is a rendering of Julian's 14th century work into English contemporary with 21st century North America. I use the term *rendering* rather than *translation*, because it is not a scholarly work. There are a number of the latter extant, especially *The Complete Julian of Norwich*, by Fr. John-Julian, OJN, published by Parakeet. This rendering is a work of simple devotion for the benefit of average folk, Mother Julian's even-Christians and their contemporaries. It is based upon the Sloane Manuscript, No. 2499 from the early 17th century, in the British Museum, with reference to Marion Glasscoe's 1976 edition of Sloane, and Fr. John-Julian's Paraclete translation of 2009. The text of this rendering is my own, however, based upon my own encounter with Julian's writing.

W.W. Melnyk

Julian of Norwich

NOTES

NOTES

Julian of Norwich

NOTES

NOTES

NOTES

Made in the USA
Monee, IL
18 March 2023

29935502R00059